Python
The Comprehensive Guide to Python Programming for Beginners: The Science of Computer Language

of information contained within this document, including, but not limited to, —errors, omissions, or inaccuracies.

Table of Contents

Introduction

Computer programming sounds scary but it really isn't. The hardest part is in choosing which of the languages you want to learn because there are so many to choose from. Python is one of the easiest of all of computer programming languages; indeed, pretty much everything you need is right there, at your disposal. All you need to do is learn how to use what the program gives you to write programs.

Python is simple; much simpler than many of the other languages and once you have learned it you will find it much easier to move on to more advanced Python or to another language altogether. Python provides you with the framework and libraries that you need to do just about anything that you want to do. If that weren't enough, Python also has a very large community full of people who just want to help you and put you in the right place.

Python is the chosen language of many different types of people – security testers, data scientists, web app developers, etc. Most of the big applications that you use on a regular basis today are written in Python, including YouTube, the largest video-sharing app in the world.

So, if you think that you want to learn how to program in Python, how to build the next big app, you've come to the right place. This book is intended to give you the basics of programming in Python; a starting point from which you can build your knowledge and your expertise. I have also included some basic projects for you to get started on as well as a few exercises for you to test your knowledge. By the end of the book, you should have a good grounding in what Python is and what it can do.

Chapter 1: What is Python and How Did It Start?

Python is what is known as object-oriented programming, or OOP for short. It is an interpreted language highly interactive and is perfect for beginners or for those who are experienced in other programming languages. Indeed, those of you that have learned to program in C language will spot straight away that there are an awful lot of similarities between C and Python.

The highlights of this language include:

- Easy to read
- Easy to learn
- Easy maintenance
- An excellent standard library
- Fully interactive
- Portable and extendable
- Packed with databases
- Excellent GUI programming

Python is used for so many things and today it is one of the most popular and important of all the open-source programming languages that are in use today. Some see it as a relatively new language but in actual fact, Python is older than Java and JavaScript. So where did it come from?

The Beginning

The origins of Python go back to December 1989. The creator was Guido van Rossum and it was begun as a hobby. Rather than being named after the constrictor snake, Python actually got its name from Monty Python's Flying Circus, the famous British comedy troupe of the eighties.

It came from a project that van Rossum worked on at the Dutch CWI research institute – the ABC language – a project that was terminated and from the Amoeba operating system. The main strength of the new language was the ease of which it was easy to extend and that it could support multiple platforms. This was vital in the days when personal computers were starting to become popular and because Python could communicate with a wide variety of libraries and file formats, it soon took off.

Throughout the nineties, Python grew and more functional programming tools were added into it. It also played a pivotal role in van Rossum's new initiative, Computer Programming for Everybody. The idea behind CP4E was to make programming accessible to everybody, not just the selected few, and to encourage basic computer and coding literacy as essential skills besides those of English and math. Because Python has such a clean syntax and is easy to read and access, it is now the go-to language for beginners to start on.

Open-Source Python

Throughout the nineties, as Python continued growing, users were concerned that it was entirely dependent on van Rossum keeping it going. What would happen to

Python if something happened to van Rossum? The solution was to make Python open-source, available to all, and to facilitate that Python 2.0 was released in 2000 by the BeOpen Python Labs team, with the idea being that it was more community oriented and a lot more transparent in the development process. It repository was moved over to SourceForge giving more people "Write" access to the CVS tree and a much easier way for bugs to be reported and patches submitted. Today, we still use Python 2.7 and it will continue to receive support until 2020. Indeed, there will be no 2.8, instead, the focus will be on Python 3, the new member of the family.

Python 3

Python 3 was finally born in 2008, not just an update but a complete overhaul. Surprisingly, there would be no backward compatibility, which meant developers would have to choose and use just one. With Python 3, the idea was to clean up house to remove duplicate models and constructs and to ensure that there was one obvious way of doing something. Despite the introduction of tools like "2to3", which would identify things in Python 2 code that had to be changed to work in Python 3, many users opted to stick with what they knew best. Even today, many years after Python 3 was released, there should be no assumption made that programmers would be using the later version.

Chapter 2: Why Use Python?

Basically, Python is the go-to programming language for just about anything you want to do. It is a general purpose programming language, used by millions of people to do all sorts of things, from testing out a microchip, building video game, even powering some of the largest web application's in the word, like Instagram and YouTube. It's a small language, it is very close to the English language and it contains hundreds of libraries for you to choose from. Apart from all that, why would you use Python? Here are three reasons:

Readability

Because Python is so close to the English language, it is easy to read. Add to that the very strict rules of punctuation in Python and it's even more readable unlike some programming languages that are littered with curly braces instead of punctuation. Python also runs by a set of rules that inform developers exactly how their code is to be formatted. Called PEP 8, the rules mean that a programmer always knows exactly where they need to put a new line in and it also means that, when you read a script written by someone else, you know that the same rules apply and you won't have any trouble reading and understanding it.

Libraries

Python has been in existence for almost 27 years and in that time an awful lot of code has been written. Because it is open source, this code is made available to every programmer to use. You can install it on your own system and use it in your projects or you can modify it for your own use. All of this code is installed in libraries and there are libraries that cover just about anything you want, from manipulating an image right up to the automating a server.

Community

Python has one of the largest programming communities and there are groups just about everywhere. Major conferences are held regularly on virtually every continent in the world, with the exception of Antarctica. There are workshops, online and offline and there are plenty of forums where you can go for help and to join in with other programmers. When you begin to learn Python, it is advisable that you join a couple of these forums and become active in them. That way, when you need help, you'll get it.

Chapter 3: Getting Started

Before you can begin to learn Python, you need to set up your environment. For users of Ubuntu and Mac OS X, Python is already installed on your system so this next part is for Windows users only. This will work on all versions of Windows from 7 right up to 10.

1. Download Python – choose from 2 or 3, whichever suits your needs.
2. Run the Python Installer and when given the option, choose **Customize Installation**
3. Click all the boxes beside all the options under **Optional Features** and click on **Next**
4. Look for **Advanced Options** on the next screen and choose the location you want to install Python to

The next step is to set up PATH variable. This will allow you to include the directories that contain all the packages and components that you will need. To do this:

- Open up Control Panel on your Windows computer
- Look for **Environment**
- Under **System Environment Variable,** click on **Edit.**
- Click on **Environment Variables**
- Look for **User Variables** and then do one of two things – edit an existing path or create a new one. To do the latter, select PATH as the variable name and add the directories that are listed under this section into the section for Variable Values. Each must be separated with a semicolon

- To edit an existing path, you must ensure that each value is on a separate line in the dialog. Click **New** and then put one of the following directories onto each line:

C:\Python35-32;
C:\Python35-32\Lib\site-packages\;
C:\Python35-32\Scripts

- You can now open a command prompt. To do this, click **Start>Windows System>Command Prompt**
- When the command prompt is open, you can type the following in:

Python

This loads the Python interpreter and you should see something similar to this:

Python 3.5.1 (v3.5.1:37a07cee5969, Dec 6 2015, 01:38:48) [MSC v.1900 32 bit (Intel)] on win 32

Type "help", "copyright", "credits" or license for more information.

>>>

Type Exit and hit the Enter key – this will take you back to your command prompt

Text Editors

Python

Python cannot be programmed without a text editor and on a Windows system, you already have one – Notepad. Do not use Word – it is not an editor and your files will not be saved correctly.

The best one to use is called Notepad ++ on Windows and Text Wrangler for the Mac. Here's how to set them up:

Windows

- Download and install Notepad ++
- Open up Settings for Notepad++ and click on **Language Menu>Tab Settings**
- Tick the box beside **Expand Tabs**
- Don't change the value, it should be 4
- Click on Close

Mac

- Download and install TextWrangler
- If a message pops up telling you that you have to register or install other software, just click **Cancel -** you don't need to do either
- Follow the on-screen instructions to set the editor up

You are now ready to move on to learning about the basic coding and functions of Python

Chapter 4: The Basics of a Python Program

I apologize in advance but this is going to be a long chapter. Please take your time over it, don't try to take it all in at once because, after a certain point, your brain ill stop taking in the information. I have included exercises for you to do along the way and the answers are at the back of the book. Repeat these exercises as often as it takes for the point to stay in your brain.

No matter which language you speak or read in, unless the words are in the right order, and have the right punctuation, they will not make sense. This also applies to Python. The interpreter with the language can easily interpret your code and run it but only if it is structured in the right way. Take this simple example, structured in a way that Python will understand and run it:

print("Hello, world!")

Just one simple line is all it takes for Python to understand and run your instruction. It isn't a good introduction to Python syntax though so take a look at this more complex example:

 # This is the main function.

def my_function():

  print("Hello, World!")

my_function()

9

It says the same thing but in a more complex way. This is known as a "skeleton" simply because you can add to it to make it more complex.

NOTE – the first line consists of just a # which is to denote the beginning of the comment. Python ignores anything between the hash and the line end. More about comments later on.

Keywords

All computer languages contain keywords. These are words that are reserved by the language for a specific purpose and you cannot use them for anything else in the program. These are the reserved keywords for Python:

- and
- as
- assert
- break
- class
- continue
- def
- del
- elif
- else
- except

- False
- finally
- for
- from
- global
- if
- import
- in
- is
- lambda
- None
- nonlocal
- not
- or
- pass
- raise
- return
- True
- try
- while
- with
- yield

Identifier names

In the course of creating a program in Python, you will create a large number of entities - variables, classes, and functions, for starters. These all have to be given a name that is unique, known as an identifier. Python has a set of rules to follow when you form an identifier:

- It must contain only letters, lower or upper case, numbers and the underscore (_) – there cannot be any spaces
- It cannot begin with a number
- It cannot be or include a keyword

If any one of these rules is broken the program will close displaying a syntax error. Not every identifier, even when correct, mean anything to a human being. These are the guidelines that should be followed when you name a variable to make it readable by the human eye:

- It must be descriptive – the name of the variable must describe what it contains; the name of a function should describe what the function actually does, etc.
- You shouldn't use unnecessary abbreviations as this can make things harder to read

Pick one convention for naming and stick with it throughout. This is one of the more common conventions:

- Class names should be written in CamelCase – each word capitalized and all words squashed together
- Where a variable is to be a constant, the name should be written in CAPITAL_LETTERS_WITH_UNDERSCORES
- All other variable names should be written in lower case_with_underscores.
- The names for methods and class attributes that are to be "private" and not accessible from outside of the class must be started with an underscore

There are exceptions to every rule. Many of the more common of the mathematical symbols tend to have shorter names but are understood widely. These are some identifiers, and how not to write them:

Syntax Error Good	Bad
Person Record PersonRecord	PRcrd
DEFAULT-HEIGHT DEFAULT_HEIGHT	Default_Ht
class AlgebraCourse	Class
2totalweight total_weight	num2

Exercise 1

Looking at the table above, write down the reason why you think entries on the left will produce a syntax error if they are used as identifiers.

Flow of Control

In the Python language, you write statements as lists in exactly the same way as you write a shopping list for example. The computer will start with instruction one and work its way through each one in the exact order they show up in the list. It will only stop once the final instruction has been completed. The order of execution is known as "flow of control".

Indentation and Semi-Colons

Mot computer languages use curly braces {} to arrange blocks of code or they use BEGIN and END statements. This is designed to encourage you to indent code blocks as a way of making for easier reading but you don't have to use indentation. Python uses it as a way of delimiting a block so you MUST indent your code:

```
# this function definition begins a new block
def add_numbers(a, b):
    # this instruction will be inside the block, because it is
indented
    c = a + b
    # as is this one
    return c


# the if statement begins a new block
if it is Tuesday:
    # the statement is inside the block
    print("It's Tuesday!")
# and this one is outside the block!
print("Print this no matter what.")
```

Many languages use a semicolon to denote where each instruction ends. However, Python uses line ends to determine where each instruction ends. You can use a semi-colon if you are going to have several instructions on one line but that is bad form:

```
# Each of these is an individual instruction – no need to
use a semi-colon!
print("Hello!")
print("Here's a new instruction")
```

```
a = 2

# This instruction spans several line
b = [1, 2, 3,
   4, 5, 6]

# This is legal, but you shouldn't really do it
c = 1; d = 5
```

Exercise 2

Write the statements that are in the block that is created by the function called *append_chickens*:
```
no_chickens = "There are no chickens here ..."

def append_chickens(text):
   text = text + " Crawwwk!"
   return text

print(append_chickens(no_chickens))
```

Exercise 3

This program hasn't been indented correctly. Write it again as it should be:
```
def happy_day(day):
if day == "monday":
return ":("
if day != "monday":
return ":D"

print(happy_day("sunday"))
print(happy_day("monday"))
```

Letter Case

Python is one of the few case-sensitive computer languages, which means that both upper and lower case letters are not treated the same as one another. For example, if you were to use "A", it would be different from "a" and the function, "def main()" is not the same as "DEF MAIN()". Also keep in mind that reserved words are all lower case, with the exception of True, False and None.

Section A: More on Comments

If you recall, a comment begins with a # and they carry on until the line ends. For example:

 # This would be a comment
print("Hello!")   *# this tells the computer to print "Hello!"*

All comments will be ignored by the Python interpreter and are used by the programmer for two things:

- To say what the program does
- To say how the program works, in more detail that the code does

You do not need to comment on each line, just where it is appropriate, i.e. in a place where it might be unclear what is happening. Some computer languages support comment that go cross several lines; Python doesn't. If you have a need to type a long comment into your program, you must split it down into a number of different lines, with a # at the beginning of each line.

Reading and Writing

Some programs will show text on your screen, to give or to request certain information. For example, you may wish to tell a person what your program actually does so you would write something like this:

Welcome to Josephine's Calculation Machine

You may want to request that the user inputs a number:

Please enter the first number:

The best way to get information output is to show a string literal that includes the *print* function. String literals are lines of text that are surrounded by quotes, single or double. It doesn't matter which you use but you must use the same one at the start and end of the string literal. These are a few examples:

"Welcome to Josephine's Calculation machine"
'Please enter the first number:'

To get the computer to print, or display the word 'Hello' on your screen you would use this instruction:

Print("Hello!")

Note that the *print* function sees the string as an argument, printing the string and printing a newline character. This explains why the cursor shows up on the next line after something has been printed.

If you wanted to ask a user for a bit of information, we would use the *input* function, as such:

first_number = input ('put the first number in)

There are a few things to take note of here. First, the *input* function doesn't automatically print a newline; the text is input immediately following the prompt. This is why, after the colon, there is a trailing space. Secondly, the function is always going to return a string as the output; it is up to you to convert it into a number. You don't have to add a parameter, you can use the *input* function without the string prompt, as such:

second_number = input()

Files

The *print* function will print to the screen by default but it can also be used to write something to a file, as such:

with open('myfile.txt', 'w') as myfile:
  print("Hello!", file=myfile)

There is a reasonable amount going on here. Where we used the *with* statement, we opened the file called *myfile.txt* to write to and then assigned it the variable called *myfile*. In the *with* block, we have written *Hello!* into the file, along with the newline character. Finally, the *w* character that we passed to *open* is indicating that the file must be opened up for writing.

We don't have to use the *print* function; we may use the *write* method in a file, like this:

with *open('myfile.txt', 'w')* **as** *myfile:*
  myfile.write("Hello!")

Methods are functions that are attached to objects – more about methods later on. The *write* method doesn't put a newline character at the end of the string.

You can use the *read* method to open a file and read the data:

```
with open('myfile.txt', 'r') as myfile:
    data = myfile.read()
```

This will read the file contents into variable *data*. This time did you spot that we passed "r" to the *open* function, which means that the file is to be opened for reading.

Built-In Types

A computer is able to process a lot of different types of information, such as characters and numbers. The types of information that Python can use are called types and the language contains a large number of common types, i.e. floating-point numbers, integers, string, etc. Programmers are also able to define types by using classes.

Types consist of two separate bits – a domain containing a possible set of values and a set that contains possible operations, both of which may be performed on any value. For example, if the domain as of type int (integer), it would only contain integer values, while the common operation for integers includes subtraction, multiplication, division and addition.

Python is what is known as dynamically typed, which means that there is no need to specify types for variables when created – the same variable can be used to store the values for different types. But, because Python is also a strongly typed language, at any one time, the variable must have a definitive type. For example, if you were to attempt to add a number into a string Python would kick up an error and exit without attempting to work out what you wanted.

Type is a function that is used for determining what type an object is, i.e.:

print(*type(1)*)
print(*type("a")*)

Integers

Integers are now as type int and are whole numbers, for example 1, 3, 5, 2587, or -256. The number 3.5 is not classed as an integer because it contains a decimal point. This makes it a floating-point number. Any number that contains a decimal point comes under this rule, even 1.0.

Integer Operations

Python is able to display integers using the *print* function but only under one circumstance – if it is the sole argument:

print(*3*)
 # Let's add two numbers together

print(*1 + 2*)
Strings and integers cannot be directly combined because of the fact that Python is a strongly typed language:

>>> **print**(*"My number is " + 4)*
Traceback (the most recent call last):

File "<stdin>", line 1, in <module>
TypeError: Cannot convert 'int' object to str implicitly

In order to print both a string and a number together, you have to first turn the number into a string:

 # str function will convert things into strings.
 # Then we can go ahead and concatenate two strings with +.
print(*"My number is " + str(4))*

 # String formatting will do the conversion for us.
print(*"My number is %d" % 3)*

Operator Precedence

One very important thing to keep in mind is operator precedence. For example, take *1+2//3*. It could mean *1+2)//3* or it could mean *1+(2//3)* Python contains a very specific way, a somewhat predictable way, in which the order of operations is determined. With an integer operation, Python will handle anything inside brackets () first, followed by ** which is followed by *, then //, then % and then +, followed by -.

If you write an expression that has a number of operations in it, all of which carry the same precedence, they are to be performed in order. If you have left-associative operators, they will be performed from left to right and right to left for right-associative operators. Just so you know, all the arithmetic operators are left associative, with the exception of the right-associative **. For example:

all of the arithmetic operators except for ** are left-associative, so
2 * 3 / 4
will be evaluated left to right:
(2 * 3) / 4

** is right-associative, so
2 ** 3 ** 4
will be evaluated right to left:
2 ** (3 ** 4)

Exercise 4

Which of these numbers are proper integers in Python?

- *110*
- *1.0*
- *17.5*
- *-39*
- *-2.3*

Write down the results of these operations and say why they are the results:

- #. 15+20*3
- #. 13//2+3
- #. 31+10//3
- #. 20%7//3
- #. 2**3**2

Strings

Strings are, in essence, nothing more than a sequence of characters and we have already talked briefly about string literals. In the Python language, a string, of type str, is a special type. They behave in much the same way as lists do but they also contain a certain functionality that is specific to text.

Formatting Strings

Sometimes you will have to print ot a message that isn't a fixed string, maybe it has values that are stored inside variables in it. There is a way to do this, by using the right syntax for string formatting:

name = "Janet"
age = 23
print*("Hello! My name is %s." % name)*
print*("Hello! My name is %s and I am %d years old." % (name, age))*

The symbols that start with % are what we call placeholders. The variables that go into the positions are placed after the %, the string formatting operator, in the order in which they were put in the string. If there is a single string, it requires no wrapper whatsoever but if there are more than 1, they must be placed into a tuple, enclosed by (). The placeholder symbols will begin with different letters, depending entirely upon the variable type. For example, *age* is an integer but *name* is a string. All of the variables are converted into string before they can be added to the rest.

Escape Sequences

Escape sequences may be used as a way of denoting special characters that are not easily typed on the keyboard. They may also be used to denote characters that are reserved for something else. For example, if you wanted to put a newline in your string you would do this:

print('This is a line.\nThis is another line.')

If the string has single quotes around it, you must escape apostrophes and you do the exact same thing for a string that is inside double quotes. Escape sequences begin with a (\) backslash, as such:

print('"Hi! I\'m Janet," she said.')
print("\"Hi! I'm Janet,\" she said.")

If one of the quotes was not escaped, it would be treated as the last quote in the string by Python and it would not parse the remaining statement and throw up a syntax error:

```
>>> print('"Hi! I'm Janet," she said.')
  File "<stdin>", line 1
    print('"Hi! I'm Janet," she said.')
                 ^
```

Raw Strings

On occasion, you will have to define a string literal that has a large number of backslashes in it and escaping each and every one of them is a long and boring job. You can get around this if you use the *raw string* notation included in

Python and to do this, you place an "r" in front of the first quote. This indicates that the string contents are exactly as you have written them and that the backslashes mean nothing in particular. An example of this will be:

 # This string will end in a newline
"Hello!\n"

 # This string will end in a backslash that is followed by an 'n'
r"Hello!\n"

Triple Quotes

We've talked of single and double quotes but sometimes you will have to use triple quotes. This will be when you need to define a literal that spans many lines or has a lot of quotes in it. To do triple quotes, you either use singles or doubles but, as usual, what you start with, you must end with. Inside the quotes, all of the whitespaces will be treated literally so, if you were to type in a newline, it would be shown in your string. Make sure you do not add anything in that you really don't want in there – everything will go into your string! These two literals will be exactly the same:

string_one = """"Hello," said Janet.
"Hi," said Robert."""

string_two = '"Hello," said Janet.\n"Hi," said Robert.'

String Operations

One of the most common string operations is concatenation, used as a way of joining a pair of strings together. The symbol for concatenation is +. There are quite a few functions built into Python that can perform a number of different operations on strings and the strings themselves also have some very useful methods. These are functions, attached to an object that can be accessed by using the attribute reference operator:

name = "Janet Smith"

 # Find out the length of a string with the len function built-in
print*(len(name))*

 # Print the string that has been converted to lower case
print*(name.lower())*
 # Print the original string
print*(name)*

In case you were wondering, the reason why the final print statement outputs the original value of name is because the 'lower' statement hasn't actually changed the value. Instead, we get a copy that has been modified but if you wanted to change that name on a permanent basis, you would need to assign the variable a new value, like this:

 # Convert this string into lower case
name = name.lower()
print*(name)*

Python strings are what is known as immutable, which means that once created, they cannot be changed. What you can do instead is assign a new value to a variable name that already exists.

Exercise 5

Write these strings with single and not double quotes and use escape sequences where necessary:

#. "Hi! I'm Eli."

#. "The title of the book is \"Good Omens\"."

#. "Hi! I\'m Sebastien."

1. Write out a string, using escape sequences, that represents three letters – A, B, C - separated with tabs

2. Write down what the output is of this statement sequence:

name = "John Smith"
print*(name.lower())*
print(name)

Now answer this question – why is the output on the second line not in lower case?

Section B: Variables and their Scope

Variables are labels that denote where in the memory something is stored and they can hold values. In a programming language that is statically typed the variables each have a predetermined value and each variable may only hold the value of that specific type. With Python, you can use one variable to store different types.

Think of a variable a being akin to the common memory function in a good calculator. It will hold a value that you can retrieve any number of times but when you store a newer value, the old one is erased. They are different from the calculator memory in the fact that you can have any number of variables storing any number of different values, each variable being referred to by it's own name.

When you define a variable in the Python language, all you do is give a label a value. For example, we could come up with a variable named *count*, containing an integer value that is zero, like this:

count = 0

Note that this is the syntax that we would use to assign a value to an existing variable of the same name. If you attempt to access values in variables that have not been defined, the Python interpreter is going to exit, giving you a "name" error.

Several variables can be defined on a single line but this is not good practice:

```
# Let's define three variables at the same time:
count, result, total = 0, 0, 0

# This is the same as:
count = 0
result = 0
total = 0
```

To stick with a good style of programming, try to have names that mean something for each of your variables.

The Scope Of a Variable and Its Lifetime

You can't access every variable from every part of your program and not every variable will last for the same length of time. Where and for how long you can access a variable depends entirely on how you defined it. The section of the program where the variable can be accessed is called "scope" and the amount of time it is available for is called "lifetime".

Variables that are defined inside the main file body are global variables and these can be seen throughout the whole file and inside a file that can import the specific file. A global variable has far-reaching effects and can cause some unintended consequences – a good reason to not use them unless absolutely necessary. You should only insert objects into the global namespace if they are going to be used globally, like classes and functions.

If you define a variable inside another variable, it will be a local variable. It can be accessed from where it was defined to where the function ends and will only exist while that function executes. The names of the parameters that are in the definition of the function act like local variables but hold values which are passed to the function as and when it is called. If you use the assignment operator (=) within a function, it will make a new local variable by default, unless there is already a variable of that name already defined within the scope.

These are some examples of variables in scopes:

```python
# This one is a global variable
a = 0

if a == 0:
    # This one stays a global variable
    b = 1

def my_function(c):

    # this one is a local variable
    d = 3
    print(c)
    print(d)

# Now we can call the function, and pass 7 as the value of
the one and only parameter
my_function(7)

# a and b still exist
print(a)
print(b)

# c and d no longer exist -- they will produce name errors
```

print(c)
print(d)

The Assignment Operator

As you have already seen, the assignment operator is an 'equals' sign (=). It is used to assign the value that is on the right of the statement to the variable that is to the left. On occasion, the variable will be created first. If the value on the right is from an expression, perhaps an arithmetic expression, the evaluation will take place before the assignment happens. Here are some examples:

a_number = 5   *# a_number is 5*
a_number = total   *# a_number is the value of the "total"*
a_number = total + 5   *# a_number is the value of the total with 5 added*
a_number = a_number + 1   *# a_number is the value of a_number with 1 added*

The statement at the end would look odd if we interpreted = to be a mathematical sign. Obviously, a number can't be the equal of the same number with one added. Remember, = is the assignment operator so the statement is going to assign the variable with a new value called a_number, the same as the initial value of a_number with one added.

When you assign the first value to the variable, it is known as initializing. Definition of a variable and value assignment are carried out in a single step in Python – in other languages, it may be done in two steps. Because of this it is very rare that you will encounter an error as such:

On the left of the assignment, there must be a valid target:

```
# this is OK:
a = 3
```

```
# but these are not OK:
3 = 4
3 = a
a + b = 3
```

Assignment statements can have more than one target, each separated by the =. The expression that is located on the right side of the final = sign is the one that will be assigned to all of the targets and each target has to be valid:

```
# a and b are both set to zero:
a = b = 0
```

```
# this is not right because 0 cannot be set to b:
a = 0 = b
```

Compound Assignment Operators

So, we know that we may assign the result of an arithmetic expression to a variable:

```
total = a + b + c + 50
```

Counting will often be done in a program. You may, for example, want to keep an total of how many times a specific action is carried out in a program and you do this using the variable named *count*. The variable could be given an initial value of zero and it would add one every time that action happens. This is the statement you would use:

count = count + 1

This is one of the most common operations and Python contains a shorthand operator, +=, which allows you to express the operation better, without the need to write the variable name twice:

 # These statements have the same meaning:
count = count + 1
count += 1

 # We can increase a variable by whatever number we want.
count += 2
count += 7
count += a + b

Conversely, Python has a similar operator, -=, that allows us to decrease by a number:

 # These statements have the same meaning:
count = count - 3
count -= 3

Crossing Boundaries with Scope

What if you were inside a function and wanted to gain access to a global variable? Well, you can do this but there are a couple of things you need to be aware of:

a = 0

def my_function():
  print(a)

my_function()

The print statement outputs a zero – this is the result of "a", which is the global variable. But have a look at this:

a = 0

def my_function():
  a = 3
  print(a)

my_function()

print(a)

When you call a function, the inside print statement will output 3 but why will the end print statement output zero. By default, the variables are created by the assignment statement in the local scope. This means that the assignment contained in the function will not make any change to the global variable; instead, it will make a new variable named "a" and give it a value of 3. The initial print statement will output the new variable value, which is local, simply because, where a global and a local variable have identical names, the local variable always takes precedence. The end print statement will provide the output of the global variable, which does not change.

If you were inside a function and wanted to change a global variable, we would use the *global* keyword:

a = 0

def my_function():
  global *a*
  a = 3
  print(*a*)

my_function()

print(*a*)
You cannot refer to a local and a global variable that have identical names from within the same function; all you will get is an error message:
a = 0

def my_function():
  print(*a*)
  a = 3
  print(*a*)

my_function()
"a" has not been declared as global so the assignment that you see in line 2 in the function will make a local variable called "a". Because of this, you now cannot make any reference to the global variable named "a" from anywhere else within the function, even if it is before this particular

line. The initial print statement will now refer to local variable "a" but there is no value in line 1 because it hasn't yet been assigned.

To be honest it is not good practice to try and access a global variable from within a function and it is definitely bad practice to attempt a modification of them. Because of this, we can't easily arrange the program we are writing into a logical order that is made up of parts that won't cause an unexpected effect on each other. Really, if the function has to have access to an external function, the value should be passed as a parameter into the function.

Exercise 6

Describe what the scope of each of these variables – A, B, C, D – is in this example:

def my_function(a):
  $b = a - 2$
  return b

$c = 3$

if c > 2:
  $d = my\_function(5)$
  print(d)

1. Using that example, write down the lifetime of the variables stating when they are going to be created and then destroyed.
2. Take a guess at what the outcome would be if you gave C a value of 1.

3. Discuss why this would cause a problem and how it could be avoided.

Modifying Values

In some computer languages, you can define a special variable that can only be given a value once which means, one the value has been set, it can't be changed. These are known as *constants*. Python doesn't allow these restrictions but we do have a convention that is widely used to ensure that certain variables are marked as an indication that the values should not change. Their names are written in CAPITAL letters and underscores separate each word:

 # These variables are known as constants by convention:

NUMBER_OF_DAYS_IN_A_WEEK = 7
NUMBER_OF_MONTHS_IN_A_YEAR = 12

 # There is nothing preventing us from redefining them...
NUMBER_OF_DAYS_IN_A_WEEK = 8

 # ...but we shouldn't really do it.
So, why would you define a variable with a value that isn't intended to change? Have a look at this:
MAXIMUM_MARK = 80

tom_mark = 58
print(("Tom's mark is %.2f%%" % (tom_mark / MAXIMUM_MARK * 100)))
 # %% is how we escape a literal % inside a string

There are a number of reasons why you would define MAXIMUM_MARK instead of just putting 80 into the print statement. Firstly, we are giving this number a label that tells us what it is, which makes your code a lot more readable and understandable. Secondly, you might want to refer to that number several times in your program. If you have to change the value for that MAXIMUM_MARK, you only need to go to one place to do it, not several, cutting down on the risk for errors.

Where you see literal numbers dotted through a program, these are called "magic numbers" and it is not good practice to do this. However, this doesn't apply to the small numbers that are really self-explanatory. You should be able to easily understand the reason why a particular total has been initialized as zero or increased by 1.

On occasion, you may want to make use of a variable as a way of distinguishing between a number of discrete option. It is best to refer to those values of the options using constants, rather than directly, especially where the value does not have any natural meaning:

```python
# We will define a few options
LOWER, UPPER, CAPITAL = 1, 2, 3

name = "Janet"
# We will use constants when we assign these values...
print_style = UPPER

# ...and when we check them:
if print_style == LOWER:
    print(name.lower())
```

```
elif print_style == UPPER:
    print(name.upper())
elif print_style == CAPITAL:
    print(name.capitalize())
else:
    # Nothing stops us from setting print_style to 4, 55 or
    # "fork" by accident, so we can put this fallback in place
just to be safe:
    print("Unknown style option!")
```

In this example, values 1, 2, and 3 have no importance and are, in fact, totally meaningless. You could use any value you like, such as 4, 5, 6, but just keep in mind that the value has to be different. If you had put the values in and not the constant, you would find that the program was very difficult to read so using strings that mean something is far better. However, it would be easy to make a mistake, say in spelling, while we were setting our values and we might not notice. This would throw up an almost instant error.

There are libraries in Python that define some of the common constants for convenience, i.e.

```
# these libaries have to be imported before we use them
import string
import math
import re
```

```
# All lower case ASCII letters:
'abcdefghijklmnopqrstuvwxyz'
print(string.ascii_lower case)
```

```
# The mathematical constants, pi and e, are floating-
point numbers
print(math.pi) # the ratio of the circumference of the
circle to the diameter
print(math.e) # natural base of logarithms

# We can pass this integer to functions in the re
# (regular expression) library.
print(re.IGNORECASE)
```

Mutable and Immutable Types

There are Python values that can be changed and some that can't. However, this doesn't mean that you are unable to change the values in variables but, if that variable has an immutable value in it, rather than changing it the only thing you can do is give it a new value.

Examples of immutable types are strings, integers and floating point numbers. Go back over the examples and you will see that when the values were changed, we actually gave them new ones using the assignment operator:

```
a = 3
a = 2

b = "Janet"
b = "Robert"
```

However, even this is not going to make any changes to the total-in-place value; it will also give a new value:

total += 4

We haven't yet covered mutable types but examples of these are dictionaries and lists. In short, a mutable type is one that can be changed. most of the objects that you will likely write yourself are mutable:

 # this is a number list
my_list = [1, 2, 3]
my_list[0] = 5 # we can modify the first element of the list
print*(my_list)*

class MyClass*(object):*
    pass *# this is a stupid class*

 # Now we can use the class as a type and create a simple object
my_object = MyClass()

 # We can also modify the values of the attributes that are on the object
my_object.some_property = 42

Input

We looked earlier at how to use the print function as a way of making a program show a message, or to use the input function as a way of reading the value of a string. However, what if you wanted to get your user to type in a number or some other type of variable? In this case, you will still make use of the input function but you still have to convert the values of the strings that are returned by the input into types that you want. Have a look at this example:

```
height = int(input("Enter the height of rectangle: "))
width = int(input("Enter the width of rectangle: "))

print("The area of the rectangle is %d" % (width *
height))
```

int is one function that we use to convert the values of a number of different types into int. However, it is vital for you to realize that int cannot convert strings that contain anything other than digits into integers. If you try to do this, the program is going to exit, displaying an error. So when you write the program it is entirely reliant on the input of a user and we all know that human errors occur. We must put some safeguard in place so that a recovery is possible in the event of an error. For example, you could put a safeguard in place that detected a bad input and would exit with a better error message than before:

```
try:

    height = int(input("Enter the height of rectangle: "))
    width = int(input("Enter the width of rectangle: "))
except ValueError as e: # if a value error occurs, we can
skip to this point
    print("Error reading height and width: %s" % e)
```

Be aware that only one attempt will be made to read the program before it exits with an error. You can ask a user to carry on inputting until the value is correct and you would do this:

correct_input = False # this is a Boolean value -- it can be true or false.

__while not__ correct_input: # this is a while loop
  __try__:
    height = int(input("Enter the height of rectangle: "))
    width = int(input("Enter the width of rectangle: "))
  __except__ ValueError:
    __print__("Please make sure you enter valid integers for both height and width.")
  __else__: # this can nly be executed if there is no value error
    correct_input = True

A bit more about this later on but first, another example – how to calculate the petrol usage of a vehicle:

What we are going to do here is write a program that asks a user to input the distance that has been traveled by a vehicle along with the total cost of the fuel bought to cover the distance. Using this, along with the cost of petrol per liter, the program is going to be able to calculate how efficient the car is, in terms of kilometers per liter and in liters per 100 kilometers. First, we have to define the price of the petrol and we do this as a constant. This is to make it easier to modify the cost as it changes:

PETROL_PRICE_PER_LITRE = 5.50
When the program begins, we want a welcome message to be printed out:

*__print__("*** Welcome to your fuel efficiency calculator! ***\n")*

 # you can add anotherblank line after the message using
\n

Now ask the user to put in their name:

name = input("Enter your name: ")

Ask how many kilometers were traveled:

float is a function that converts values into floating-point numbers.

distance_travelled = float(input("Enter distance travelled in km: "))

Ask the user how much it cost:

amount_paid = float(input("Enter the value of the fuel that you bought for your trip: R"))

Now we can run the calculations:

fuel_consumed = amount_paid /
PETROL_PRICE_PER_LITRE

efficiency_l_per_100_km = fuel_consumed /
*distance_travelled * 100*
efficiency_km_per_l = distance_travelled /
fuel_consumed

Lastly, we can see the results:

print("*Hi, %s!*" *% name*)
print("*Your car's efficiency is %.2f litres per 100 km.*" *%*
efficiency_l_per_100_km)
print("*This means that you can travel %.2f km on a litre*
of petrol." *% efficiency_km_per_l*)

 # we can also add an extra blank line before the message using \n
print("\nThanks for using the program.")

Exercise 7

1. Write a program that will convert a Fahrenheit temperature to Celsius. Assume that T_c = (5/9) x (T_f - 32), where T_c is the Celsius temperature and T_f is the Fahrenheit temperature. Your program will ask for a value for the input and then print the result as an output; both input and output should be in floating point numbers:
2. Now discuss what could cause this program to crash and what would you do to make it work better?

Type Conversion

As you gain more experience and write programs, you will begin to find that, on occasion, you will need to do conversions on data types, perhaps you need to convert a string into an integer or maybe an integer into a floating point number. Python allows two different types of conversion – explicit and implicit.

Implicit Conversion

We know that we are able to combine an integer and a floating point number in an arithmetic expression. The result of an expression like this is always going to be a floating point number. The reason for this is that Python converts the integers into floating point numbers and then it evaluates the expression. This is called an implicit conversion – in other words, you don't do any converting, Python does it for you.

The following example shows how the integer 2 is converted into a floating point number:

result = 8.5 * 2

2 is the int type while 8.5 is the float type. Python converts operands automatically so that they are the same type. In this particular case, we achieve that only if the int 2 has been converted into a floating point equivalent, in this case, 2.0. Then we multiply the floating-point numbers.

This is a more complicated example of the same principle:

result = 8.5 + 7 // 3 - 2.5

Python will perform its operations going on the precedence order and decides, for each operation, whether a conversion needs to take place or not. In the example we have used, // takes precedence and, as such, is processed first. There are two integers here, 7 and 3 and the integer division operator is //. The result from this particular operation is 2, which is of int type.

The rest of the operation is 8.5 + 2 – 2.5. Both subtraction and addition are of the same precedence and, as such are evaluated from the left to the right, beginning with the addition. First, we convert 2 into a floating point number, 2.0, and then we add the floating point numbers together. The result of that is 10.5 – 2.5 and the end result is 2.0.

Section C: Explicit Conversion

When you convert a float to an int, there will always be some loss to the precision. If, for example, you were to try converting 5.834 into an int, you would find that you wouldn't be able to do it without losing some precision. If you want this to happen, you have to tell Python, explicitly, that you know the precision is going to be lost. This example shows a floating point number being converted into an int:

i = int(5.834)

We use the int function to convert floats to ints by getting rid of the fractional section – be aware that the number will always be rounded down, never up. If you want to have more control on how the number is rounded, you will have to use another function:

 # the floor and ceil functions are found in the math module
import *math*

 # ceil is always going to return the closest integer that is greater than or equal to the number
 # (it will always round up)
i = math.ceil(5.834)

 # floor will return the closest integer that is less than or equal to the number
 # (it will always round down)
i = math.floor(5.834)

```
# round will return the closest integer to the number
# (it will round up or down)
# This is a built-in function and we don't need to import
math to use it.
i = round(5.834)
```

Converting to and from Strings

As we have seen, Python will very rarely perform an implicit conversion to or from the type str. You would have to do the conversion explicitly. If you were to pass a value over to the print function, it would be converted to a string automatically but if you attempt to add together a string and a number, you will see an error message:

```
# This one is OK
print(5)
print(6.7)
```

```
# This one isn't OK
print("3" + 4)
```

```
# Did you mean to put this...
print("3%d" % 4) # concatenate "3" and "4" to get "34"
```

```
# Or maybe this?
print(int("3") + 4) # add 3 and 4 to get 7
```

If you wanted to convert a number to a string, you should use string formatting as this is the best way of inserting several values into one message. If you wanted to convert one number into a string, you would use the str function in an explicit way:

```
# These lines are all going to do the same thing
print("3%d" % 4)
print("3" + str(4))
```

Conversions

In the Python language, functions such as float, int, and str, will attempt to convert anything into its respective type. For example, you could use the int function as a way of converting a floating point number into an integer or a string to an integer. Please note that, while an int is able to convert floats to integers, it cannot directly convert strings that contain floats into integers:

```
# This one is OK
int("3")
```

```
# This one is also OK
int(3.7)
```

```
# This one is not OK
int("3.7") # This string representation is of a float, not of an integer!
```

```
# We must convert the string into a float first
int(float("3.7"))
```

Bool type values can contain one of two values – True or False. Both of these values are used quite a lot in conditional statements. These will either execute or not execute a part of your program, dependent on certain binary conditions:

my_flag = True

***if** my_flag:*
  ***print**("Hello!")*

The condition is usually an expression which is evaluated to a Boolean value:

***if** 3 > 4:*
  ***print**("This will not be printed.")*

That said, pretty much any value can be converted implicitly to a Boolean, provided it is used in a similar way to this statement similar:

my_number = 3

***if** my_number:*
  ***print**("My number is non-zero!")*

Normally, this would behave exactly as you would think it would – a zero is False and a non-zero is True. However, when it comes to strings you must exercise caution – empty strings are seen as False and anything else, even a "False" or "0" string will be treated as True.

 # bool is a function that we use to convert a value to a Booleans
bool(34) # True
bool(0) # False
bool(1) # True

bool("") # False
bool("Janet") # True
bool("o") # True!
bool("False") # Also True!

Exercise 8

1. Convert 8.8 into a float.
2. Convert 8.8 into an integer (with rounding up or down).
3. Convert 8.8 into an integer (with rounding up or down).
4. Convert 8.8 into a string.
5. Convert 8 into a string.
6. Convert 8 into a float.
7. Convert 8 into a Boolean.

Selection Control Statements

As a finale to this brief look at Python coding, we are going to look at selection control statements. These are a big part of coding and something that you need to get the hang of if you are going to be successful. We've already looked flow of control, i.e. the sequence in which the computer will execute statements. Normally, a computer program will execute the instructions in the exact order they are written but this isn't always going to be true. In order to change how the computer does this, we use selection control statements.

These are used to let the program choose which order and when specific instructions should be executed. For example, the program can choose which direction to go in based on what a user inputs. As you can see, these statements are intended to give a computer program more versatility.

if Statement

Every day you make decisions and each of those decisions is based on certain criteria. For example, your choices for lunch may be based on how you feel at that particular time or whether you are having to follow a specific diet. Once you make the decision, you will act on it and this is what makes decision-making a two-step process.

The same is true when a computer program needs to make a decision and, in Python, these decisions will be made using the *if* statement, also called the selection statement. When your program processes an *if* statement, it will first look at certain criteria or conditions. If these can be met, the action will be carried out. The syntax we use for this statement is:

if condition:
  if_body

When a program comes to an *if* statement, the instructions are only going to be carried out if the condition is true. Look at this example:

if age < 18:
  print("Cannot vote")

The instructions that are in the *if* part can only be executed if the related condition is true. If it can't be met or is false, then the program will skip over the instructions contained in in the *if* statement

Relational Operators

In order to make a decision, some *if* statements will compare two values. Look at the previous example – we compared the value of the integer 18 to the variable *age* to see if the age was lower than 18. The operator < was used to carry out the comparison – this is a relational operator, one of a number included in Python. These are the other relational operators that are included:

Operator Example	Description	
==	equal to	*if*
(age== 21)		
!=	not equal to	*if*
(score != 12)		
>	greater than	*if*
(num_people > 45)		
<	less than	*if*
(price < 30)		
>=	greater than or equal to	*if*
(total >= 60)		
<=	less than or equal to	*if*
(value <= 25)		

Be aware that a condition statement can be true or false. Also keep in mind that the operator used for equality is ==, a double equals sign. Remember from earlier that = is the assignment operator so, if you were to use = instead of ==

by accident, you would more than likely get a syntax error kicked up.

```
>>> if choice = 3:
File "<stdin>", line 1
  if choice = 3:
     ^
SyntaxError: invalid syntax
```

This is correct:

```
if choice == 3:
    print("Thank you for using this program.")
```

Value and Identity

Up until now, we have used integers for comparison in the examples but you can use any relational operators in comparing strings, floating point numbers, and other data types:

```
# we can compare the values of strings
if name == "Jane":
    print("Hello, Jane!")

# ... or floats
if size < 10.5:
    print(size)
```

When we use == to compare variables, what we are doing is a value comparison, i.e. checking to see both the variables contain the same value. In direct contrast, we might also want to see if two objects, like dictionaries, lists or custom objects that you have created are exactly the same This is called a test of identity and while two objects might have the exact same contents, they could be different objects. To compare identity, we use the *is* operator:

```
a = [1,2,3]
b = [1,2,3]

if a == b:
    print("These lists contain the same value.")

if a is b:
    print("These lists are the same.")
```

Generally, if two variables do happen to be the same object then, by the same token, they are equal. However, the reverse isn't equal – while two variables can be the same value, they may not be the same object. As a way of testing if two objects are not the same, we would use the *is not* operator:

```
if a is not b:
    print("a and b are not the same object.")
```

Using Indentation

So far, in the examples in this section, we have used just one statement in the *if* body but you can have several in there if you want:

```
if choice == 1:
    count += 1
```

print("Thank' for using this program.")
print("Always print this.") # this is outside of the if block

The Python interpreter will treat every statement that appears inside the indented block as a single statement, processing all the instructions inside that block before going on to the next statement. This means that we can specify several instructions that have to be executed when the condition of the *if* statement is met.

In Python, *if* is a compound statement. This is because it can combine several statements together. Compound statements contain one or more clauses. Each clause has its own header and a suite, or list of statements. We use indentation to delimit the suite contents and, to put them in the same block, each line has to be indented to the same level.

Section D: The Else Clause

One part of a statement that is optional is the *else* clause and it is used to let us specify alternative instructions that are to be executed in the event the condition hasn't been met.

if condition:
  if_body
else*:*
  else_body

In other words, if the condition is true, the program will execute the *if* body; if the condition is false, the *else* body will be executed. Look at the next example, showing the *if else* statement at work. In this case, if the condition is met, 1 will be added to x provided it is zero; if it isn't met, 1 will be subtracted:

if x == 0:
  x += 1
else*:*
  x -= 1

Exercise 9

1. Write down which of the following fragment are valid or invalid first line of an if statement and then explain your reasoning for the invalid lines:

if (x > 4)
if x == 2
if (y =< 4)

```
if (y = 5)
if (3 <= a)
if (1 - 1)
if ((1 - 1) <= 0)
if (name == "Jenny")
```

2. Write down the output of this code fragment and then explain your answer:

```
x = 2
3.
if x > 3:
print("This number")
print("is greater")
print("than 3.")
```

3. How can the following code fragment be simplified?

```
if bool(a) == True:
print("a is true")

if x > 50:
b += 1
a = 5
else:
b -= 1
a = 5
```

Nested *if* Statements

On occasion, you may require a certain decision to depend entirely on an earlier result. For example, you may need to choose a certain shop to go to, but only if your earlier decision was that you were going to go shopping. In Python, this is the equivalent of placing an *if* statement inside the body of an *if* or an *else* clause that is attached to a different *if* statement. The following example shows you the code fragment that is calculating how much it will cost to send a small package. The post office has a charge of R5 for 300g. R2 is then charged for every 100 g after that rounded up, to 1 kg or 1000 g.

```
if weight <= 1000:
    if weight <= 300:
        cost = 5
    else:
        cost = 5 + 2 * round((weight - 300)/100)

    print("Your parcel is going cost R%d." % cost)

else:
    print("Maximum weight for small parcel has been exceeded.")
    print("Use the large parcel service instead.")
```

Did you spot that the outer *if* and *else* clauses have been indented? Also, note that the inner *if* and *else* clause bodies have been indented again. You must keep track of the indentation to ensure that each of your statements is in the correct block. It makes no difference if there is an empty lie in between the final line of the inner *if* statement and the print statement because they are still in the same block – they have been indented by exactly the same amount. Empty lines can be used to make code a bit more readable but don't overdo it.

if Ladders and the *elif* Clause

When you add the *else* keyword in, you will be able to specify certain actions for cases where the condition is not met or is false. However, there will be cases where you want more than two alternatives to be handled.   An example of the code using nested *if* statements might look a little like this:

```
if mark >= 80:
   grade = A
else:
   if mark >= 65:
      grade = B
   else:
      if mark >= 50:
         grade = C
      else:
         grade = D
```

OK, so this isn't the easiest of codes to read. Each time you add in a nested *if* statement, the indentation has to be increased and that means each alternative has a different indentation. The code can be better written like this:

```
if mark >= 80:

   grade = A
elif mark >= 65:
   grade = B
elif mark >= 50:
   grade = C
else:
   grade = D
```

Now each alternative is a clause of a single *if* statement and they are all indented the same. We call this an *if* ladder.

We can also add in a default condition, the *else* clause. If none of the conditions that you specified earlier can be matched, then the actions that are inside the *else* body is executed. Always include an *else* clause at the end of each ladder so that all cases have been covered. This is especially important if there is any chance that the options are likely to change somewhere down the line. Look at this code:

```
if course_code == "CSC":
    department_name = "Computer Science"
elif course_code == "MAM":
    department_name = "Mathematics and Applied Mathematics"
elif course_code == "STA":
    department_name = "Statistical Sciences"
else:
    department_name = None
    print("Unknown course code: %s" % course_code)

if department_name:
    print("Department: %s" % department_name)
```

So, what would happen if you came across an informatics course? It would have a code of *INF.* What would happen is the *else* clause is executed and you would see a message printed out that tells you the course is not supported. But, if you were to omit the *else* clause, you wouldn't have spotted that there was anything wrongg until you attempted to use *department_name*. Then you would find out that a value had not been assigned to it. By making sure you use the *else* clause you can pick up on any potential problems straight away.

Boolean Values, Operators, and Expressions
The Bool Type

The Python programming language contains a value type for all variables that can be true or it can be false – that type is called the Boolean type, or *bool*. The false value of bool is *False* and the true value is *True*. If you use a value type like a Boolean, then Python will convert it to a Boolean. An example of this would be a condition of an *if* statement. You will rarely need to cast a value explicitly to bool and you will also not need to use the == operator exploit either in order to check if the value of a variable evaluates to *True*. Instead, you can use the name of the variable on its own as a condition:

name = "Janet"

 # This is shorthand for checking if name evaluates to True:
if name:
  print("Hello, %s!" % name)

 # It means the same thing as this does:
if bool(name) == True:
  print("Hello, %s!" % name)

 # This won't give us the answer that we expect:

```
if name == True:
    print("Hello, %s!" % name)
```

Look at the code carefully and ask yourself why the final *if* statement is not doing what you expect it to. If you cast the string called *Janet* to a Boolean, you will see that it is equal to *True* but, while it is a string, it won't be equal to *True*. This is why the final *if* statement evaluates to *False*. This is the reason why you should use shorthand syntax as you can see in the initial statement – Python will do any implicit casts for you.

NOTE

0 and 0.0 are equal to *False* while 1 and 1.0 are equal to *True*. However, do not mistake them as identical objects. To test them out, use the *is* operator.

Boolean Operations

Often, we base decisions on several factors, for example, you would choose to purchase a skirt on the conditions that you like it **and** it is priced lower than R100. Alternatively, you may opt to go out for dinner if you have nothing in the fridge to eat **OR** you really don't feel up to cooking anything.

You can also change a decision by negating it. You may decide that you will go to the cinema tomorrow night only if it is **NOT** raining. You can join conditions that have simple conditions together using AND NOT and OR. These conditions are known as Compound Conditions and the operators are called Boolean operators.

Chapter 5: Three Basic Projects of Python

For this chapter, I am going to give you three projects to have a go at. I will discuss what is in them and I will give you a couple of hints along the way as well as providing you with the correct code or possible solutions to the projects. Don't cheat; don't look for the answers before you have a good go at doing them yourself.

Project 1

I want you to create a program that will request a user to put in their name and their age. Print a message that tells the user, based on the information they provide, what year they will turn 100 years old.

When you have done that, add on to your program by asking that the user gives you a number that will tell you how many copies of the message you will print. (*Hint – don't forget the order of operations*)

Finally, print the requested number of messages on separate lines. (*Hint – using the string "\n will do the same as pressing Enter*)

User Input in Python

When you want to ask a user to input something in Python, your code will use the command, *input()*. The result is stored in a variable and can then be used as much as you want. Keep in mind that, no matter what a user input, even a number, the result is going to be a string. An example of that:

name = input("Tell me your name: ")
print(*"Your name is " + name*)

The result printed out on your terminal or shell (depending on operating system you are running Python in, will be:

>>> Tell me your name: Michael
*Your name **is** Michael*

What is happening here is that after *input()*, the program is waiting for the user to input something, to type in their answer and then press the ENTER key. The program will not go any further until that ENTER key has been pressed.

Manipulating strings

The result you will get from your *input()* function will be a string so what do you do with it? First, you must convert the string to a number. Let's assume that you are completely and utterly positive that the user is inputting a number. The string can be converted to an integer using the function *int()*. This should look something like this:
age = input("Enter your age: ")
age = int(age)
(or, if you want to be a little cleaner with your code)
age = int(input("Enter your age: "))

So, in both cases, *age* is going to hold a variable and that variable will be an integer. With that, you can now do math. A note here; you can also do the opposite, i.e. turn integers into strings by using the *str()* function.

Second, you can do Math with strings. By that, I mean that if you wanted to combine, or concatenate, as the correct computer term is, strings, all you have to do is add them together:

print(*"Were"* + *"wolf"*)
print(*"Door"* + *"man"*)
print(*"4"* + *"chan"*)
print(str(4) + *"chan"*)

And the same will work if you wanted to multiply them:

print(4 * *"test"*)

However, you cannot do subtraction or division like this. For multiplication, the thought of multiplying a pair of strings together hasn't really been all that well defined. What does it actually mean to multiply these strings? It does make a kind of sense in terms of specifying the multiplication of a string by a number – all you do is repeat the string as many times as you need to multiply it. Have a go at this in your own code, using all of the available arithmetic operators with strings and numbers. This is absolutely the best way to see what works and what doesn't work.

Sample Solution to Project 1

name = input("What is your name: ")
age = int(input("How old are you: "))

year = str((2014 - age)+100)
print(name + " will be 100 years old in the year " + year)

Project 2

For this project, I want you to create a program that asks a user for a specific string and then prints whether the string is a palindrome. For those that don't know, a palindrome is a string that will read exactly the same forwards and backward.

List Indexing

In most computer programming, and most definitely in Python, when you start to count list, they begin from the number 0. The very first element of any list will "number 0", the second will be "number 1", and so on. As a result of this, when you need to retrieve a single element from a list, you ask the list to give you that number element:

```
>>> a = [5, 10, 15, 20, 25]
>>> a[3]
20
>>> a[0]
5
```

You can also use this very convenient method to get a sublist in between a pair of indices

```
>>> a = [5, 10, 15, 20, 25, 30, 35, 40]
>>> a[1:4]
[10, 15, 20]
>>> a[6:]
```

[35, 40]
>>> a[:-1]
[5, 10, 15, 20, 25, 30, 35]

The very first number is called the "start index" and the very last number is called the "end index". A third number may also be included in the indexing as a way of counting the number of times you should read from this list:

>>> a = [5, 10, 15, 20, 25, 30, 35, 40]
>>> a[1:5:2]
[10, 20]
>>> a[3:0:-1]
[15, 10, 5]

In order to read the entire list, you would use the variable name which, in these examples, is "a" or you put [:] after the variable name, for example, "a[:]"

A String is a List

Because a string is actually a list, you can do all the things to a string that you would do to a list. For example, you could iterate through a string:

string = "example"
for *c* **in** *string:*
  print *"one letter: " + c*

Which will give this result:

one letter: e
one letter: x

one letter: a
one letter: m
one letter: p
one letter: l
one letter: e

You can also take sublists:

>>> string = "example"
>>> s = string[0:5]
>>> print s
exam

Which gives variable "s" a string called "exam"

Sample Solutions for Project 2:

Using String Reversal

```
wrd=input("Please enter a word")
wrd=str(wrd)
rvs=wrd[::-1]
print(rvs)
if wrd == rvs:
   print("This word is a palindrome")
else:
   print("This word is not a palindrome")
```

Using *for* Loops

```
def reverse(word):
      x = ''
      for i in range(len(word)):
```

```
    x += word[len(word)-1-i]
    return x

word = input('give me a word:\n')
x = reverse(word)
if x == word:
    print('This is a Palindrome')
else:
    print('This is NOT a Palindrome')
```

Project 3

Write a program or function that will take a list and then return you a new list. The new lit will have all of the elements from list 1 without any of the duplicates in it. To do this, write two separate functions – one that uses a loop and constructs the list and another that uses a set.

Sets

In terms of Math, sets are collections of elements in which no element is ever repeated. This is useful because you will know that all of the elements stored in a set will be completely unique.

Set Features:

- Sets are in no particular order, meaning there won't be a "first" or "last" element. You will not be able to ask a set to give you the "nest" element
- There are absolutely no repeats in a set, all items are unique
- Conversion between sets and lists is very easy

In Python programming, you use the *set()* keyword to make a set and use it. For example:

```
names = set()
names.add("Michael")
names.add("Robert")
names.add("Michael")
print(names)
```
The output is:
```
set(['Michael', 'Robert'])
```

You can pretty much do to a set what you can do to a list, with the exception of asking for specific numbered elements. You can convert a list to a set and a set to a list easily:

```
names = ["Michael", "Robert", "Sarah", "Michael"]
names = set(names)
names = list(names)
print(names)
```
The result is:
```
['Michael', 'Robert', 'Sarah']
```

Sample Solutions for Project 3

I am going to show you sample solutions for the two different functions that allow you to do this project in two ways – with a loop and with sets:

Using the *for* loop

```
# this one uses a for loop
```

Python

```
def dedupe_v1(x):
  y = []
  for i in x:
   if i not in y:
    y.append(i)
  return y
```

Using Sets

```
#this one uses sets
def dedupe_v2(x):
  return list(set(x))

a = [1,2,3,4,3,2,1]
print a
print dedupe_v1(a)
printdedupe_v2(a)
```

Conclusion

First of all, I would like to thank you for taking the time to read my book. It is by no means a comprehensive lesson on coding but I hope that I have been able to give you the basics, enough for you to be able to move on and expand your learning.

The thing about computer programming is that your learning will never stop. Even if you think that you have the basics down pat, if you don't use what you have learned regularly, believe me when I say that you will soon forget it! Computer programming is evolving on an almost daily basis and it's up to you to keep up with everything that is going on. To that end, you would be well advised to join a few of the Python communities. You will find many of these on the internet and they are places where you can stay up to the minute with changes, where you can join in conversations, discuss code and ask for help. Eventually, you will be in a position of being able to help the newbies on the scene and it is then that you will realize just how far you have come.

So, where do you go from here? The first thing to do is go over this book as many times as necessary to let the content sink in. Don't just read it once and think that you know it all because you don't. The human brain can only take in so much information in one go and it needs time to assimilate that information and store it away before the next influx. Trying to take in pages and pages of code and information will not serve you well and it isn't a case of being the quickest to read it. You can read as much as you like but, once your brain stops taking the information in, you anything else will be meaningless.

Take your time; do the exercises as many times as you need to until you know that you can write the answers AND understand the answers in your sleep. That is important – it is not enough to know the answers with Python programming. You have to be able to understand WHY the answer is such, the process that gets to that answer if you don't understand the code from start to finish you will never be able to understand the answers.

From here, once you understand the principles behind programming, behind the different bits that make up a Python code you can move on to the more advanced concepts of programming. There are a few ways you can do this:

- Purchase another book, one that takes you further into the concepts of Python programming
- Take an online course. There are a lot of Python programming courses online so do your research and find one that suits your level of learning and teaches you everything you want to know. Some of these courses are supplied free of charge, while others do as you to pay for the course. I can't say which one is best but do choose one that comes from a recognized source rather than an unheard of one that you found on page 53 of the Google searches
- Go back to college. Check out your local colleges and universities for Python programming courses. Many of these are likely to start in the fall and will

teach you everything you need to know with an instructor on hand to answer your questions.

So, these are three very different learning course and which one you take will depend entirely on how you feel more comfortable learning about Python and taking your knowledge further. Don't force yourself to learn in a way that is not comfortable for you because I can guarantee that you will not learn anything.

Once again, I would like to take this opportunity to thank you for your time. The only real advice I can give you at this stage is this – practice, practice, practice. It really is the only way. Write programs for fun just to see if your understanding of the concepts is correct. Write programs just to see what works and what doesn't – it's one thing being told that something doesn't work but there is no experience like seeing it for yourself, on the screen, because that way you will understand WHY it doesn't work.

I would like to wish you well in your Python programming and I hope that I have been able to give you at least a good head start.

Answers to Exercises

Exercise 1

Syntax Error	Reason
Person Record	The identifier has a space in it
DEFAULT_HEIGHT	The identifier contains a dash
class	The identifier is a keyword
2totalweight	The identifier begins with a number

Exercise 2

There are two statements in the block that are defined by the function *append_chickens.* They are:

text = text + " Crawwwk!"

return *text*

Exercise 3

Correctly indented, the code would look like this:

def happy_day(*day*):
  if *day* == *"monday"*:
    return *":("*
  if *day* != *"monday"*:
    return *":D"*

print(*happy_day("sunday")*)
print(*happy_day("monday")*)

Exercise 4

1. The correct integers are 110 and -39
2. Results of the operations and reasons why:

- 15 + 20 * 3: 75 - * is of the higher precedence than +
- 13 // 2 + 3: 9 - // is of the higher precedence than +
- 31 + 10 // 3: 34 - // is of a higher precedence than +
- 20 % 7 //3: 2 - // and % are equal in precedence but are both left-associative. The left operation will be performed first
- 2 ** 3 ** 2: 512 - ** is right associative so the one furthest on the right will be performed first

3. A ZeroDivisionError will be raised

Exercise 5

1. The single quoted strings would be:
   - #. 'Hi! I\'m Eli.'
   - #.'The title of the book is "Good Omens".'
   - #. 'Hi! I\'m Sebastien.'
2. The single quoted string would be "a\tb\tc"
3. The output will be
   - john smith
   - John Smith

The reason why the second output is not in lower case is because a Python string is immutable and the function *name.lower()* will return a brand new string that contains the lower case name.

Exercise 6

1. In the scope of *my_function*, *a* is a local variable. This is because it is actually the name of an argument. *B* is a local variable also inside

my_function simply because it has been assigned a value in the function. Both *c* and *d* are global variables, despite the fact that *d* has been created side the *if* block. This is because inside an *if* block is not classed as being a new scope – the contents of the block are part of the same scope as that on the outside of the block. The only things that can indicate a new scope level are class definition, beginning with *class* and function definitions which start with *def*.

2. Whenever *my_function* is called, *a* and *b* will be created. They will both be destroyed when *my-_function* has completed execution. *C* will be created whenever it is assigned the value of 3 and will exit for as long as the program is executing. When assigned a value that is returned from the function, *d* will be created inside the *if* block and it too will remain for the duration of the execution.

3. If *c* were given a value of that was not more than 3, the *if* block could not be executed. The knock-on effect of that would be that *d* could not be created.

4. The variable could be used later on in your code, provided it exists. If it didn't exist, the program would crash. It is not considered to be good coding style to define or undefine a variable depending entirely on what the outcome of a conditional statement is. It is best to ensure that a variable is always defined, regardless. You could assign it a default value to begin with if you wanted because it is far easier to check if a variable has a default value than to see if it even exists.

Exercise 7

1. A sample program would be:

T_f = float(input("Please enter a temperature in °F: "))
*T_c = (5/9) * (T_f - 32)*
print("%g°F = %g°C" % (T_f, T_c))

2. The program may crash if an entered value cannot be converted into a floating point number. You would have to add in something that would check for errors to ensure this couldn't happen, perhaps by storing a string value and then checking over its contents. If the value entered is not valid you can do one of two things – print out an error message and exit or continue to prompt the user to carry on inputting values until the right one goes in.

Exercise 8

1. a_1 = float("8.8")
2. a_2 = math.round(8.8)
3. a_3 = math.round("8.8")
4. a_4 = "%g" % 8.8
5. a_5 = "%d" % 8
6. a_6 = float(8)
7. a_7 = bool(8)

Exercise 9

Answers:

1. if (x > 4) – valid
2. if x == 2 – valid (brackets are not compulsory)
3. if (y =< 4) – invalid (=< is not a valid operator; it should read <=)
4. if (y = 5) – invalid (= is the assignment operator, not the comparison operator)
5. if (3 <= a) – valid

6.   if (1 - 1) – valid (1 - 1 evaluates to zero, this is false)
7.   if ((1 - 1) <= 0) – valid
8.   if (name == "Jenny") – valid

  1. The program is going to print:

is greater
than 3.

The last two if print statements in the code have not been indented and are outside of the *if* statement. This means that they are always going to be executed.

  2. We do not need to compare variables to Boolean values and then to *True* explicitly. If we evaluate the variable that is in the *if* statement condition, this will be done implicitly.

if *a:*
    print*("a is true")*

A is set to the same value regardless of whether the *if* block or the *else* block is executed so this line can be moved outside of the *if* statement and only has to be written once:

```
if x > 50:
    b += 1
else:
    b -= 1
    a = 5
```

Made in the USA
San Bernardino, CA
09 December 2016